النصرانية - الأصل الواقع

CHRISTIANITY
The Original and the
Present Reality

By

Dr. Muhammad bin Abdullah As-Saheem

Translation and Footnotes

Abdul-Qaadir Abdul-Khaaliq

DARUSSALAM

DARUSSALAM
GLOBAL LEADER IN ISLAMIC BOOKS
Riyadh • Jeddah • Al-Khobar • Sharjah
Lahore • London • Houston • New York

In the Name of Allâh
the Most Gracious, the Most Merciful

"And there is none of the people of the Scripture (Jews and Christians) but must believe in him ['Îsâ (Jesus), son of Maryam (Mary), as only a Messenger of Allâh and a human being] before his ['Îsâ (Jesus) عليه السلام or a Jew's or a Christian's] death (at the time of the appearance of the angel of death). And on the Day of Resurrection, he ['Îsâ (Jesus)] will be a witness against them." (*Sûrat An-Nisâ'*, 4:159)

النصرانية - الأصل الواقع

CHRISTIANITY

The Original and the
Present Reality

© **Maktaba Dar-us-Salam, 1996**

King Fahd National Library Cataloging-in-Publication Data

As-Saheem, Dr. Muhammad bin Abdullah

Christianity the original and the present reality-
Riyadh.

32p., 14x21 cm. ISBN 9960-740-52-8

I-Islam   I-Title

210. dc.   1424/3591

Legal Deposit no. 1424/3591

ISBN 9960-740-52-8

Headoffice: P.O. Box: 22743, Riyadh 11416 K.S.A. Tel: 00966-01-4033962/4043432 Fax: 4021659
E-mail: darussalam@awalnet.net.sa Website: http// www.dar-us-salam.com

K.S.A. Darussalam Showrooms:

Riyadh

Olaya branch:Tel 00966-1-4614483 Fax: 4644945

Malaz branch: Tel 4735220 Fax: 4735221

- **Jeddah**
  Tel: 00966-2-6879254 Fax: 6336270
- **Al-Khobar**
  Tel: 00966-3-8692900 Fax: 00966-3-8691551

U.A.E

- Darussalam, Sharjah U.A.E
  Tel: 00971-6-5632623 Fax: 5632624

PAKISTAN

- Darussalam, 36 B Lower Mall, Lahore
  Tel: 0092-42-724 0024 Fax: 7354072
- Rahman Market, Ghazni Street
  Urdu Bazar Lahore
  Tel: 0092-42-7120054 Fax: 7320703

U.S.A

- Darussalam, Houston
  P.O Box: 79194 Tx 772779
  Tel: 001-713-722 0419 Fax: 001-713-722 0431
  E-mail: sales@dar-us-salam.com
- Darussalam, New York
  572 Atlantic Ave, Brooklyn
  New York-11217, Tel: 001-718-625 5925

U.K

- Darussalam International Publications Ltd.
  226 High Street, Walthamstow,
  London E17 7JH, Tel: 0044-208 520 2666
  Mobile: 0044-794 730 6706 Fax: 0044-208 521 7645
- Darussalam International Publications Limited
  Regent Park Mosque, 146 Park Road,
  London NW8 7RG Tel: 0044-207 724 3363
- Darussalam
  398-400 Coventry Road, Small Heath
  Birmingham, B10 0UF
  Tel: 0121 77204792 Fax: 0121 772 4345
  E-mail: info@darussalamuk.com
  Web: www.darussalamuk.com

FRANCE

- Editions & Librairie Essalam
  135, Bd de Ménilmontant- 75011 Paris
  Tél: 0033-01- 43 38 19 56/ 44 83
  Fax: 0033-01- 43 57 44 31
  E-mail: essalam@essalam.com

AUSTRALIA

- ICIS: Ground Floor 165-171, Haldon St.
  Lakemba NSW 2195, Australia
  Tel: 00612 9758 4040 Fax: 9758 4030

MALAYSIA

- E&D Books SDN. BHD.-321 B 3rd Floor,
  Suria Klcc
  Kuala Lumpur City Center 50088
  Tel: 00603-21663433 Fax: 459 72032

SINGAPORE

- Muslim Converts Association of Singapore
  32 Onan Road The Galaxy Singapore- 424484
  Tel: 0065-440 6924, 348 8344 Fax: 440 6724

SRI LANKA

- Darul Kitab 6, Nimal Road, Colombo-4
  Tel: 0094-1-589 038 Fax: 0094-74 722433

KUWAIT

- Islam Presentation Committee
  Enlightment Book Shop
  P.O. Box: 1613, Safat 13017 Kuwait
  Tel: 00965-244 7526, Fax: 240 0057

INDIA

- Islamic Dimensions
  56/58 Tandel Street (North)
  Dongri, Mumbai 4000 009,India
  Tel: 0091-22-3736875, Fax: 3730689
  E-mail:sales@IRF.net

SOUTH AFRICA

- Islamic Da'wah Movement (IDM)
  48009 Qualbert 4078 Durban,South Africa
  Tel: 0027-31-304-6883
  Fax: 0027-31-305-1292
  E-mail: idm@ion.co.za

CONTENTS

5

Publishers Note

All the praise is due to Allâh, Who has guided us to His straight path. We seek His forgiveness and we seek refuge in Him from the evil of our own selves and our bad deeds.

'Christianity – the Original and the Present Reality' is a brief treatise in which the author has attempted to open the Christians' eyes to the true reality of their erroneous beliefs and to guide them to the Truth.

All the Messengers of Allâh had tried their best, to convey the correct creed to their peoples. Prophet 'Isa, or Jesus, was also among those upright Messengers who strove hard to guide his people to the truth, but most of them followed their whims and desires and thus went astray.

Believing in the Oneness of Allâh is a basic fundamental in Islam. This belief establishes the relationship between human beings and their *Rubb* (Lard). As Muslims we firmly believe that Allâh is our Creator, Sustainer and the true God; only He has the right to be worshipped. There is no partner with Him. He has the free hand in the disposal of all affairs.

I pray to Allâh to render this booklet beneficial and to be a source of guidance and blessing in both this world and the Hereafter.

I am thankful to Br. Muhammad bin 'Abdullah As-Saheem who has written this booklet in the Arabic language and given us permission to translate it into English. I also appreciate Darussalam's staff, who spared no effort to complete this work in a very good manner.

Abdul Malik Mujahid
General Manager
Darussalam

Introduction

All praises and thanks are due to Allâh, Who has not taken any creature as a son, nor does He have any partner in His dominion, nor has He any protector from among the lowly creatures. His Greatness is greater than all else. I bear witness that there is nothing worthy of worship in truth besides Allâh Alone Who is singular and without partner, and I bear witness that Muhammad ﷺ[1] is His slave, servant and Messenger.

This is a very brief summary in which I intend to clarify the origin of Christianity (*Nasraaniyah*) and its current reality. It is principally intended for the Christian in order that he may be aware of the roots of his belief. He will perhaps come to understand how Christianity has undergone change and substitution to the point that it has evolved into a man — made composition – this, after

---

[1] *Sallallâhu 'alaihi wa sallam* – It is the transliteration of the invocation made by Muslims upon mentioning the name of Prophet Muhammad. It is commonly translated as "Peace and Blessings be upon him" or "Peace be upon him". Though this rendering is correct in part, it does not fully convey the meaning which is explained in the commentary on the verse "Verily Allâh and His angels *yusalloona 'alan-Nabiy.* O you who believe *salloo alaihi wa sallimoo tasleema*". The full meaning of this passage and the epithet is long and difficult to concisely convey while simultaneously giving it full justice in the English language. It would more closely be explained as meaning: "May he (Prophet Muhammad) be mentioned in the heavens by Allâh and His angels and given the best of salutations." And Allâh knows best. (The Book of *Tafsir, Sahih Al-Bukhari*)

having once been a Divine message. I have made it a point to bring forth, within this summary, those evidences that brought forth the truth of the matter from actual texts of the Torah (*Tawrah*) and the Injeel [1]. This was done to illustrate, to every Christian reader, my intention to point out the truth and to guide towards that which is correct. Thus I write, seeking Allâh's help.

---

[1] Commonly translated and understood as the Gospels though it literally refers to the Scripture revealed to Prophet Jesus ('Iesa) عليه السلام.

The Origin of Christianity

The origin of Christianity is like that of other Divine revelations such as the messages of Noah (Nuh), Abraham (Ibrahim) and Moses (Musa) عليهم السلام.[1] Every divinely revealed message is unanimous in its fundamental religious creed such as: Belief in Allâh as Singular and Alone and without any associate; Belief that He was neither born nor does He give birth[2]; Belief in Angels and the Day of Judgement in the Hereafter; Belief in Divine predestination, and the good and bad of it; Belief in the Messengers and Prophets.

There is nothing in recorded history, since the time of Adam عليه السلام up through the last of the Prophets, Muhammad ﷺ, indicating that any known Divine revelation differs in these beliefs. Indeed, the differences found among them are connected to the forms of worship and their various conditions or appearance. Also, those

---

[1] *Alaihimus salaam* - It is the transliteration of the invocation (plural form) made by Muslims upon mention of any of the Prophets and Messengers. Though similar in wording and meaning to the invocation made upon Prophet Muhammad, it can more simply be understood as "Peace be upon them" [singular عليه السلام*Alaihis salâm* "Peace be on him"]. Also the name *As-Salaam* (peace) is a perfect attribute of Allâh which may therefore render another meaning to the invocation that "Allâh - Who is Peace and the Grantor of security and peace to His creation - be with the Messenger or Prophet." And Allâh knows best.

[2] There being nothing before Him nor does He have any need for progeny.

things that were forbidden or permitted differed for various reasons as legislated by Allâh to the Prophets, each of whom was ordered to explain and clarify the law to the respective peoples.

Therefore, [original] Christianity can be termed as a Divine message that calls for Belief in Allâh as Singular and without associate, and that He is neither born nor does He have offspring. It confirms that Allâh indeed sends Messengers and Prophets from among men whom He has chosen from the best of people. This, in order that no one can have any argument before Allâh after having thus been sent a Messenger.

The question that one is obliged to ask is: Has Christianity remained in the state in which it was originally revealed by Allâh to His servant and Messenger Jesus ('Iesa عليه السلام)?

In order to answer this question, it is necessary to bring out for our mutual benefit, the reality of Christianity today and compare it with what has been transmitted in both the Torah and the Gospels attributed to Moses and Jesus عليهم السلام respectively. This is in order to examine: Is the present state of Christianity in accord with the original message or does it differ? Do the texts attributed to these Prophets support the beliefs that the current Christian nation stands upon? Does what is related in these books about the life of Jesus عليه السلام correspond to the image introduced in the churches of today as to the personality and character of the Messiah? – A personality which has become mythical in its proportions to the point that it can hardly be accepted in the mind or proven to be real. Such beliefs are as follows:

1. Christ, the Messiah: "Son of Allâh"

'The belief of the Christians that the Messiah is the Son of God (Allâh).'

This is a belief that is not supported by any statement of the Messiah عليه السلام. In fact, we find the Torah and the Gospels filled with evidence, to the contrary, that nullifies this belief. We find in the Gospel of John 19:6,8: "When the chief priests and the officers saw him, they cried out, 'Crucify him, crucify him!' Pilate said to them, 'Take him yourselves and crucify him, for I find no crime in him.' The Jews answered him, 'We have a law, and by that law he ought to die, because he has made himself the Son of God.'"[1]

Matthew begins his Gospel C: 1:1, with what is said to be Jesus's family lineage where he (Matthew) states: "The Book of the Lineage of Christ, the son of David, the son of Abraham." In this lineage is an evidence of his being a flesh and blood mortal in contradiction to the claim of his being divine. It is as if you were to say to me, "It has been attributed to Jesus the description 'Son

---

[1] Unless otherwise noted, all biblical references are from: The Holy Bible containing the Old And New Testaments, revised standard version, translated from the original tongue being the version set forth A .D. 1611 revised A. D. 1881-1885 and A. D. 1901 compared with the most ancient authorities and revised A. D. 1952, published by Thomas Nelson & Sons. [How strange indeed that what is offered by a proof by those who insist upon the authenticity of biblical texts is such an obvious proof against themselves!]

of God', so he therefore claimed to be the Son of God." I respond thus: This description related in your book is given not only to other Prophets but to nations and peoples. It is not something peculiar to the Messiah. To be sure you can look for example in Exodus 4:22, Psalms 2:7, Chronicles 22:9-10 Matthew 5:9, Luke 3:38, and John 1:12. In all of these verses are descriptions of the aforementioned groups as "Sons of God," nevertheless they were not elevated to the level that you have given to the Messiah عليه السلام.

In the Gospel of John 1:12, we are given a definition of what is meant by the "Son of God." It shows that it means 'a believer in Allâh' as in the passage – "He came to his own home, and his own people received him not [1], But to all who received him, who believed in his name, he gave power to become children of God who were born, not of blood nor of the will of the flesh nor of the will of man, but of God."

---

[1] Referring to Jesus عليه السلام.

2. Christ: Second Element of the Holy Trinity

'The belief of the Christians that Jesus عليه السلام is a god along with Allâh, but he is the second element of the Holy Trinity.'

If we examine the New Testament in order to find the basis upon which this belief is founded, we do not find any statement that can be attributed to the Messiah عليه السلام, where he makes any such claim. We are, on the contrary, surprised to find that the New Testament contains what actually amounts to a rejection of this belief. It proclaims unambiguously and with utmost clarity that there is no God other than Allâh and that the Messiah عليه السلام is but a Messenger of Allâh sent to the Children of Israel (the Jews) confirming what was contained in the Torah and the revelation (Al-Injeel) sent through him. Here are some of the texts that support what I have just stated:

A. Jesus عليه السلام states in the Gospel of Barnabas[1] 94:1: "And having said this, Jesus said again: 'I confess before heaven, and call to witness everything that dwelleth upon the earth, that I am a stranger to all

---

[1] This Book is considered a part of the Apocrypha, i.e., those books found to be inconsistent with the official doctrine of the church and were therefore removed from the Bibles of Catholics and Protestants ready today! It can however, still be found in separate collections of Apocrypha which are comprised of several books. These collections themselves may vary, further illustrating the point that to maintain the authenticity of biblical texts is futile.

that men have said of me, to wit, that I am more than a man. For I am a man, born of a woman, subject to the judgement of God; that live here like as other men, subject to common miseries.'"[1]

B. Luke and Cleophus testify to the humanity and mortality of the Messiah when they state: "Then one of them, named Cleʻopus, answered him,[2] 'Are you the only visitor to Jerusalem who does not know the things that have happened there in these days?' And he said to them, 'What things?' And they said to him, 'Concerning Jesus of Nazareth, who was a Prophet, mighty in deed and word before God and all the people,'" Luke 24:18,19. Look also at Luke 7:17 and at Acts of the Apostles 2:22.

C. There is the statement of the Messiah عليه السلام: "And this is eternal life, that they know Thee the only true God, and Jesus Christ whom Thou hast sent." John 17:3.[3]

You can see that Christ عليه السلام, in the first text, bears

---

[1] The Gospel of Barnabas, Abul Qasim Publications

[2] The context of this story is that Jesus عليه السلام is himself the questioner having arisen but they could not recognize him!

[3] It is noteworthy that in the immediately preceding verses Jesus refers to Allâh as Father and himself as Son. This actually illustrates one of the most problematic type of contradictions in the Bible and the problem of using it as either a support or refutation of itself. Namely, one can read a statement indicating the singularity of the Creator only to be immediately followed or preceded by that which nullifies that singularity!

witness before the heavens and calls to witness all that lives on the earth that he is absolved of those attributes which elevate him above his mortal status. What can this be other than that he was no more than a human being?

In the second text, two of his contemporaries testify that he was but an honest man of God in word and deed.

While in the third text is a resounding declaration of the greatest truth in this universe which accords everlasting happiness to the one who declares it. Namely, the acknowledgement that Allâh is the only true God and anything falsely worshipped otherwise is utterly spurious and false. It is an affirmation that Christ was the Messenger of Allâh.

3. The Divine as one with Humanity

'The belief that the Divine has mixed with the human.'

If we take a close look at the teachings of Christ عليه السلام, we would see that he never directs anyone to this. On the contrary, we witness his teaching to have belief in monotheism (*Tawheed*)[1] pure from any of the stains of polytheism (*Shirk*). A very clear proof are the words of Christ related in Mark 12:29: "Listen, O Children of Israel, the Lord God is but a Single Lord." May be your perusal of the evidences I have referred to in the previous passages, along with the one I have just shown, will show you whether those evidences taken from your own Holy Book support this belief or do they conflict with it and nullify it?

---

[1] Allâh being One and Alone and singularly deserving worship and devotion.

4. Allâh is a Holy Trinity

'The belief that Allâh is an element of the tripartite commonly known as "The Holy Trinity."'

This is a belief held by Christianity alone among all Divine religions. Is it truly supported by the Holy Book or does it refute such a belief? One, who honestly gives thought to what is purported from Christ عليه السلام, will find that the basis of the message of Jesus is a call to *Tawheed* [1] and a negation of attributing to Allâh the similitudes with His creation. It is stripping away of Divine qualities from all else besides Allâh and an affirmation that worship belongs to Allâh Alone. Look again closely at the evidence cited in the second and third passages and you will not find any ambiguity or vagueness therein. This is from one point of view. A second is that Christendom has fabricated its claim that Allâh is the third of a co-equal Trinity: The Father being a God; The son a second; and the Holy Spirit a third.[2] This is incorrect. They believe that the Holy Spirit emanates from the Father and the Son. It is not possible that each element could be equal and without a beginning if the third proceeded from the two before it! As well, each single element has its own peculiar characteristics

---

[1] Pure monotheism.

[2] It is well-known that even Christians are not in unanimous agreement as to the exact nature of this Trinity. For example, some believe the Holy Spirit to be Mary, the mother of Jesus, while some others maintain it to be the Archangel Gabriel!

which cannot be attributed to the other. Also, the Father is always at the top of the scheme, with the Son after, and the Holy Spirit as the third in order. You would never accept that the Holy Spirit be placed at the fore, with the Son to follow, and the Father as the third. Indeed you would consider this as disbelief and apostasy. So how then can they be at all equal! Looking from even another angle, to even term the Spirit alone as "Holy" points to a lack of equality.

5. The Crucifixion

'The belief of the Christians that Christ was crucified by the Jews at the order of Pontius Pilate and that he died on the cross.'

The Holy Book itself provides the refutation of this belief. For in your book the one crucified is deemed accursed as is shown is Deuteronomy (22:23). "And if a man has committed a crime punishable by death and he is put to death, and you hang him on a tree, his body shall not remain all night upon the tree, but you shall bury him the same day, for a hanged man is accursed by God; you shall not defile your land which the Lord your God gives you for an inheritance." Think about it! How can your god be cursed by your very own book?

As in the Gospel of Luke 4:29,30 where Allâh safeguarded and protected the Messiah عليه السلام from the deception of the Jews and their plotting so that they were unable to crucify him: "And they rose up and put him out of the city, and led him to the brow of the hill on which their city was built, that they might throw him down headlong. But passing through the midst of them he went away." And it says in John 8:59: "So they took up stones to throw at him; but Jesus hid himself, and went out of the temple."[1] Also in John 10:39: "Again they tried to arrest him, but he escaped from their hands."

---

[1] The version which the author cites states that Jesus عليه السلام did so "Passing through the midst of them and, thus, went away."

These texts – and there are many like them – confirm that Allâh protected Christ عليه السلام from the conspiracy of the Jews and their plotting. Indeed, there are texts which confirm that the Jews were not even sure of Christ's identity to the extent that they had to hire someone to point him out to them. (See Matthew 27:3,4[1])

Likewise, Christ عليه السلام said that the disciples would be stricken with doubt on the night of his being betrayed, for he stated: "And Jesus said to them, 'You will all fall away; for it is written: I will strike the shepherd, and the sheep will be scattered.'" (Mark 14:27)

Then what indeed was the end of Christ عليه السلام upon this earth? Allâh raised him unto Himself, and this is written in your book: "And when he said this, as they were looking on, he was lifted up, and a cloud took him out of their sight. And while they were gazing into heaven as he went, behold, two men stood by them in white robes, and said, 'Men of Galilee, why do you stand looking into the heaven? This Jesus, who was taken up from you unto heaven.'"(Acts 1:9-11)[2] Also: "… for it is written, 'He will give His angels charge of you,' and 'On their hands they will bear you up…'" (Matthew 4:5,6).

---

[1] The text read.: "When Judas, his betrayer, saw that he was condemned, he repented and brought back the thirty pieces of silver to the chief priests and the elders, saying, 'I have sinned in betraying innocent blood.' They said, 'What is that to us? See to it yourself.'" He afterwards commits suicide.

[2] This is related as happening after the resurrection.

Additionally, this is related in Luke 4:10,11.[1]

Did you not see how your book conveyed the following facts?

1. That whosoever is hanged from a tree is accursed.

2. That Allâh safeguarded Christ عليه السلام and protected him from crucifixion.

3. That Christ said that the disciples would be uncertain on the night of his betrayal.

4. That Allâh raised him to heaven.

Now, to you I raise this question: For what reason is the cross considered as a holy object in Christianity while simultaneously being the place of Christ's torture – as you believe? Is it not the remembrance of an offense? Is it not a symbol of the crime and its instrument? Furthermore, do you not see that the crucifixion, as connected with Christ عليـه السـلام has no historical or religious basis to which it can be authentically attributed? Why are you so preoccupied with it to such an extent and why is so much importance placed upon it within your belief?

If you remain content with these beliefs then honestly answer the following questions:

• Who is it that controlled the heavens and the earth when their lord was tied to the wood of the cross?

---

[1] The text reads: "... for it is written, 'He will give his angels charge of you, to guard you,' and 'On their hands they will bear you up, lest you strike your foot against a stone.'"

- How conceivable is it that for three days the universe could continue without a god in control and maintaining its stability?

- Who is it that controls such enormous planets and subjects them as He so wills?

- Who is it that gives life and causes death and who uplifts or debases whosoever He wills?

- Who is it that provides sustenance to mankind and livestock?

- How was the state of the whole universe when its "lord" was in his grave?

- Who caused his "death" and who then restored him to life?

- How tremendously far above is Allâh from what they maintain![1]

---

[1] It is difficult for a Muslim translator to interpret these passages without a tremendous sense of fear at mentioning what is implied by these beliefs. Such must have been the case for the author when posing the questions and doing his research. We must seek refuge in Allâh from such ideas!

6. Christ died on the Cross

'The belief that Christ died on the cross in order to rid and erase from humanity its inherited sins.'

This belief, despite its illogicality and irrationality, contradicts the basic fundament and major texts contained within your book. Such are as follows:

1. Progenitors are not killed in substitution of their descendants.

2. Everyone dies with his own sin.

3. The offending soul dies.

4. Allâh accepts the repentance of those who sincerely repent.

The texts that support these fundamentals are:

1. "The fathers shall not be put to death for the children, nor shall the children be put to death for the fathers." (Deuteronomy 24:16)

2. "In those days they shall no longer say: 'The fathers have eaten sour grapes, and the children's teeth are set on edge.' But every one shall die for his own sin; each man who eats sour grapes, his teeth shall be set on edge." (Jeremiah 31:29,30)

3. "Yet you say, 'Why should not the son suffer for the iniquity of the father?' When the son has done what is lawful and right, and has been careful to observe all my statutes, he shall surely live. The soul that sins shall die.

The son shall not suffer for the iniquity of the son; the righteousness of the righteous shall be upon himself and the wickedness of the wicked shall be upon himself. But if a wicked man turns away from all his sins which he has committed and keeps all my statutes and does what is lawful and right, he shall surely live; he shall not die; none of the transgressions which he has committed shall be remembered against him; for the righteousness which he has done shall live." (Ezekiel 18:19-22)

7. The Lord's Supper (The Eucharist)[1]

In all that is related in the Gospels of Matthew and Mark on the story of the Lord's Supper, there is nothing that is joined with any command of Christ عليه السلام that makes this a continual act of worship or religious ritual. You can refer to the story as related in these two Gospels and you will find it as I have stated.

However, where Paul relates that it should be taken as a continual ritual, we find the additional statement: "And when he had given thanks, he broke it, and said, 'This is my body which is for you. Do this in remembrance of me.'" (I Corinthians 11:24)

This is the root of Christianity and its present reality, and this reality – as you have seen – has no link to the Messiah عليه السلام as established by any verifiable chain. The only link is that it carries the name of Christ, whereas it fails the slightest historical or religious investigation. Indeed, the "Holy Book" of Christianity contains texts attributed to the Messiah that contradict and refute the basic beliefs and important principles on which the Christian religion is laid.

The thinking person is one who disdains falsehood and hates deceit. You should be intent on becoming one of those thinkers who has renounced this profound state of

---

[1] The Last Supper with the disciples when Christ is purported to have stated the famous injunction to drink of his blood and eat of his flesh.

25

affairs and who took every hardship and difficulty in searching for the truth, demanding evidence with the desire to get to the reality of the matter.

So, I say: I shall stick to your book that will guide you if you give thought to the truth and what is correct. Do you not say in your prayer: "Hallowed be thy name. They kingdom come..." [Matthew 6:9,10]. Are you up to now waiting and saying: "Thy kingdom come"? Has that kingdom not yet arrived? For if the kingdom has come and indeed been realized, why do you still make this entreaty in your supplication?

The kingdom has surely come and reached its realization with the arrival of the Prophet who the Messiah عليه السلام himself informed us of when he said: "But the Counselor,[1] the Holy Spirit, whom the Father will send in my name, he will teach you all good things, and bring to your remembrance all that I have said to you." (John 14:26) He also said: "But when the Counselor comes, whom I shall send you from the Father, he will bear witness to me." (John 15:26). Who is it to bear witness to the message of the Messiah عليه السلام and declare him free from what the Jews fabricate about him other than the information about the Messenger of Allâh, Muhammad صلى الله عليه وسلم?

Christ also said: "I have yet many things to say to you,

---

[1] The Paraclete. Originally from the Greek word Parakletos which literally denotes "The one who is most praiseworthy." Which is equivalent to the Arabic word احمد Ahmed which is the name of Muhammad صلى الله عليه وسلم.

26

but you cannot bear them now. When the Spirit of Truth comes, he will guide you into all the truth; for he will declare to you the things that are to come. He will glorify me, for he will take what is mine and declare it to you." (John 16:12-14)

Muhammad صلــى الله عليــه وسـلم is indeed the Paraclete (the Comforter) to whom Christ عليــه السـلام pointed to. His message of Muhammad صلى الله عليه وسلم went forth. The idols fell beneath his feet (see Isaiah 42:17)[1], and his message was general to all the earth. Humanity found happiness in him and thousands upon thousands believed in him and joined him from among mankind. Be one of them and achieve true happiness in this world and in the Hereafter.

So, how do you become one of those followers of Muhammad صلى الله عليه وسـلم to achieve for yourself what his followers achieved? Indeed, this is a simple matter, All that you need to do is cleanse, purify, and rid your body of all traces of things impure and afterwards make the two part declaration أشهد أن لا إله إلا الله و أشهد أن محمدا رسول الله: *Ashhadu an la ilaha illallâh, wa ashhadu anna Muhammadar Rasulullah.*" Know the requirements of that declaration, while understanding its meaning – that there is nothing worthy of worship in truth except Allâh and that He is Alone in His right to be worshipped and obeyed and that He is the Creator and Sustainer. Also that Muhammad is the Messenger of Allâh and therefore follow and obey

---

[1] The text of which reads: They shall be turned back and utterly put to shame, who trust in graven images, who say to molten images, "You are our gods."

him in what he has ordered and believe in what he has informed us of. You must stay away from those things which he forbade us from and rebuked us for. Testify that Jesus was a servant of Allâh, and the Messenger and a word from Him as bestowed upon Mary, and a spirit[1] from Him. Also that Paradise is a reality as is Hell, and that Allâh will raise the dead from their graves. If you make this a reality in your life then you will be welcomed to become of those inheritors of the Garden of Paradise who are with the Prophets, the truthful ones, the martyrs, and the righteous.

If you would like even more writings and references to point you toward the truth and guide you to the Straight Path, for you is a list of some of the books authored by some Christian clergymen whom Allâh has guided to Islam. They have written in these books why they moved from Christianity to Islam along with the reasons that caused them to leave Christianity. They include those proofs and evidences by which they were guided to know that Islam is the Final and Everlasting Message.

---

[1] Arabic word روح *Ruh* which is usually translated as spirit or soul and occasionally causes some confusion as to the correct belief regarding Prophet 'Iesa عليه السلام. This may be the case especially in light of the Christian belief that Jesus is part of a Trinity containing the Holy Spirit. The term *Ruh* in reference to 'Iesa عليه السلام is like the souls of other creatures except that 'Iesa عليه السلام indeed holds a special status in this *Ruh* being attached to the Name of Allâh Himself. It does not imply that 'Iesa عليه السلام is at all a part of Allâh any more than when Allâh refers to the whole of the heavens and the earth as His, does it mean that they a are a part of Him or vice versa.

Bibliography and References of Books of Some Christians Who accepted Islam.

1. Religion and State by Ali bin Rabbin At-Tabri.

2. Faithful Advice on exposing the Reality of the Religion of Christianity by Nasr Bin Yahya Al-Mutatabbib.

3. Muhammad in the Holy Book, published in Arabic and English by the Ministry of Islamic Law in Qatar.

4. The Gospel and the Cross, by David Benjamin Kaldani, who accepted Islam and adopted the name Abdul-Ahad Dawood.

5. Muhammad صلـى الله عليــه وســلم in the Torah and the Gospels and the Qur'ân.

6. Forgiveness in Islam and Christianity by Ibrahim Khalil Ahmed, a former Christian minister whose name before Islam was Abraham Phillips.

7. Allâh: One or Three?

8. Christ: Human Being or God? By Magdy Morgan.

9. The Secret of My Islam by Fuad Al-Hashimi.

10. The Radiant Lighthouses in the Pitch Darknesses of this World by the guided Muhammad Zakiud-Deen An-Najjar.

This is blessed group who has chosen truth over falsehood and guidance over misguidance. Do you consider yourself more knowledgeable of Christianity than them? Then why have you not asked yourself about the reasons that lead them to abandon their former religion and declare their migration to Islam? What are those proofs and arguments which they read that drove them towards guidance and light?

I say to you that this blessed group is not the only one which left its religion and declared its Islam. They are indeed but a few of those learned Christians who have accepted Islam. I have mentioned them to you just as an example. There are many others like them and we witness caravans of faith in their daily travels on their way towards Islam, proclaiming that there is no deity except Allâh and Muhammad صلى الله عليه وسلم is the Messenger of Allâh.

Our final prayer is: all praises and thanks are to Allâh, the Lord of all the worlds.

Some Qur'ânic Verses about the Prophet Muhammad ﷺ

Allâh the All-Mighty say:

"O mankind! Verily, there has come to you the Messenger (Muhammad ﷺ) with the truth from your Lord. So believe in him, it is better for you. But if you disbelieve, then certainly to Allâh belongs all that is in the heavens and the earth. And Allâh is Ever All-Knowing, All-Wise." *(Sûrat An-Nisâ', 4:170)*

"Say (O Muhammad ﷺ): O mankind! Verily, I am sent to you all as the Messenger of Allâh — to Whom belongs the dominion of the heavens and the earth. Lâ ilâha illa Huwa (none has the right to be worshipped but He). It is He Who gives life and causes death. So believe in Allâh and His Messenger (Muhammad ﷺ), the Prophet who can neither read nor write (i.e., Muhammad ﷺ), who believes in Allâh and His Words [(this Qur'ân), the Taurât (Torah) and the Injeel (Gospel) and also Allâh's Word: "Be!" — and he was, i.e., 'Îsâ (Jesus) son of Maryam (Mary), عليهما السلام], and follow him so that you may be guided." *(Sûrat Al-A'râf, 7:158)*

"Muhammad (ﷺ) is the Messenger of Allâh. And those who are with him are severe against disbelievers, and merciful among themselves. You see them bowing and falling down prostrate (in prayer), seeking Bounty from Allâh and (His) Good Pleasure. The mark of them (i.e., of their Faith) is on their faces (foreheads) from the traces of prostration (during prayers). This is their description in the Taurât (Torah). But their description in the Injeel (Gospel) is like a (sown) seed which sends forth its shoot, then makes it strong, and becomes thick and it stands straight on its stem, delighting the sowers, that He may enrage the disbelievers with them. Allâh has promised those among them who believe (i.e., all those who follow Islâmic Monotheism, the religion of Prophet Muhammad ﷺ till the Day of Resurrection) and do righteous good deeds, forgiveness and a mighty reward (i.e., Paradise)." (*Sûrat Al-Fath*, 48:29)

"Muhammad (ﷺ) is not the father of any of your men, but he is the Messenger of Allâh and the last (end) of the Prophets. And Allâh is Ever All-Aware of everything." (*Sûrat Al-Ahzâb*, 33:40)

"Say (O Muhammad ﷺ to polytheists, pagans): Call upon those whom you assert (to be associate gods) besides Allâh, they possess not even an atom's (or a small ant's) weight either in the heavens or on the earth, nor have they any share in either, nor there is for Him any supporter from among them." (*Sûrat Saba'*, 34:22)

"And We have not sent you (O Muhammad ﷺ) except as a giver of glad tidings and a warner to all mankind, but most of men know not." (*Sûrat Saba'*, 34:28)

"Say: 'Tell me! If this (Qur'ân) is from Allâh and you deny it, and a witness from among the Children of Israel ('Abdullâh bin Salâm رضى الله عنه) testifies that this Qur'ân is from Allâh like [the Taurât (Torah)], and he believed (embraced Islâm) while you are too proud (to believe).' Verily, Allâh guides not the people who are *Zâlimûn* (polytheists, disbelievers and wrong-doing)." (*Sûrat Al-Ahqâf*, 46:10)

"And (remember) when 'Îsâ (Jesus), son of Maryam (Mary), said: 'O Children of Israel! I am the Messenger of Allâh unto you, confirming the Taurât [(Torah) which came] before me, and giving glad tidings of a Messenger to come after me, whose name shall be Ahmad.' But when he (Ahmad, i.e. Muhammad ﷺ) came to them with clear proofs, they said: 'This is plain magic.'" (*Sûrat As-Saff*, 61:6)